GREETINGS, CHAMPIONS!

About this Study Guide

Do you dream of winning a school spelling bee, or even attending the Scripps National Spelling Bee? *Words of the Champions* is the official study resource of the Scripps National Spelling Bee, so you've found the perfect place to start. Prepare for a 2021 or 2022 classroom, grade-level, school, district, county, regional or state spelling bee with this list of 4,000 words.

All words in this book have been selected by the Scripps National Spelling Bee from our official dictionary, Merriam-Webster Unabridged (http://unabridged.merriam-webster.com).

Words of the Champions is divided into three difficulty levels, ranked One Bee (900 words), Two Bee (2,075 words) and Three Bee (1,025 words). These are great words to challenge you, whether you're just getting started in spelling bees or if you've already participated in several. At the beginning of each level, you'll find the *School Spelling Bee Study List* words. For any classroom, grade-level or school spelling bee, study the 150-word One Bee *School Spelling Bee Study List*, the 150-word Two Bee *School Spelling Bee Study List* and the 150-word Three Bee *School Spelling Bee Study List:* a total of 450 words.

Following the *School Spelling Bee Study List* in each level, you'll find pages marked "Words of the Champions." Are you a school spelling bee champion or a speller advancing to compete beyond the school level? Study these pages to make sure you're prepared to do your best when these words are asked in the early rounds of competition. And remember, although spelling bees will start with words from this guide, they often end with words you haven't studied.

Each year, the Scripps National Spelling Bee will release a new version of *Words of the Champions* featuring 800 new words, including an all-new *School Spelling Bee Study List*.

Your spelling bee journey starts now, and taking the first step toward becoming a star athlete of the English language makes you a *Champion*. These *Words* are for you.

About the Scripps National Spelling Bee

The Scripps National Spelling Bee is the nation's largest and longest-running educational program. The purpose of the Scripps National Spelling Bee is to help students improve their spelling, increase their vocabularies, learn concepts and develop correct English usage that will help them all their lives. Visit spellingbee.com for more information about the Bee and to check if your school is enrolled. The Scripps National Spelling Bee is administered on a not-for-profit basis by The E.W. Scripps Company.

Difficulty Level: One Bee

School Spelling Bee Study List

wide

part

mink

tummy

goods

nook

jelly

slow

tufts

cold

lane

son

same

much

deer

silk

cove

thing

try

duckling

mask

hike

car

rage

gift

very

last

well

mess

left

rush

gone

drill

meet

lid

lisp

post

bent

mice

rope

logs

hat

swim

read

upon

idea

singing

kites

feet

must

turning

wanted

sprung

zoomed

large

closed

plates

matching

track

chart

bread

clock

crusts

pain

loud

flapped

cell

cheese

beak

cog

poor

power

foam

clutch

knife

place

oil

gushed

china

stopped

also

floor

frames

studied

spikes

speech

shoe

prize

smug

rapids

slide

goals

shelter

creak

gutter

booth

frankly

knot

search

crouched

found

gloves

pretty

baskets

bonnet

rodeo

salad

cousin

camera

wrenches

goggles

inflate

single

polish

dolphin

skiing

Texas

mumble

direct

detail

alas

barrels

clerks

forty

embers

paddles

whiskers

condition

slumped

blurted

wallet

focus

circus

aware

mango

firmly

imagined

reveal

ached

fabric

detour

impolite

squiggles

because

teachers

ordinary

capture

feline

gusto

kitchen

Difficulty Level: One Bee

Words of the Champions

gradual

ferocious

frequently

permission

towel

sundae

ornament

rooster

scold

organza

fragile

galaxy

complaint

curries

tennis

grumbling

garlic

hula

reactionary

muscular

drizzle

accurate

studio

illusionist

genetic

levity

moisture

toughness

tasteless

astute

turtle

Pinkerton

fortune

sluggard

bedlam

shortfall

cowlick

opinionated

slogan

triumphant

parenthetic

listener

guardian

dwindled

fraught

sturdy

treadmill

originate

**forfend

OR forefend

eavesdrop

January

scruple

moxie

winnow

incentive

admirer

emotional

chia

raspberry

bogus

**preferred spelling

recoup

bookworm

veteran

erase

downcast

spinal

demolition

gargantuan

salsa

chaotic

shrimp

mandate

turret

pigeon

satellite

parasite

favorite

OR *favourite

cascade

dandelion

famous

*chiefly British spelling

pristine

golden

modesty

amphibian

jealousy

remedial

vouch

trivia

shoulder

zebra

butterscotch

apron

beagle

kidney

wistful

raven

fructose

Amazon

companion

panorama

gimmick

flannel

cucumber

McMansion

janitor

lionize

headdress

ludicrous

pear

system

pedigree

empty

amulet

guess

magician

carrot

meteor

distraught

freight

honeybee

blemish

crumpet

blizzard

squirm

harmonious

lawyer

valiant

purse

raisin

trumpet

bias

lettuce

shamrock

Americana

monopolize

water

marathon

omission

newbie

spreadsheet

badger

fortification

hydra

grouse

manta

astonish

fashionista

stubble

genius

nuance

stencil

penguin

freckle

blooper

misconception

lambkin

chowder

sunflower

lambasted

volumetric

flattery

simmer

whisk

bathtub

fantastically

failure

tolerable

mosquito

target

angora

snippet

ascribe

hodgepodge

verbiage

nephew

imbibe

savvy

reckon

boorish

tarmac

iteration

nurture

volcano

forensics

miraculous

trendy

permafrost

iceberg

cactus

nationalism

leeway

pilferer

rollicking

quart

lactose

domineering

onion

abandon

vault

junior

hamlet

jubilant

thawed

uncle

dawdle

mogul

troll

kindred

tantrum

science

cement

venomous

plaintiff

mayhem

thicket

gymnastics

island

peacenik

ounce

memorandum

bother

missile

munchkin

banana

furnace

foothills

tongue

caterpillar

wasp

kudos

alpha

shebang

tibia

hazelnut

votive

storm

mince

bubbly

graham

headlong

timber

medallion

maximum

clover

casino

distinctive

mister

warning

useful

difficult

mischief

talent

kiwi

publish

mutter

sedentary

divine

lexicon

bristle

daresay

owlishly

criminal

recipient

strong

canteen

aviation

lucky

rocket

reflect

scent

puzzles

scumble

extinct

jersey

trapezoid

dillydally

haggle

sword

mastiff

cooperate

merchandise

melted

apology

carnival

buffoonery

intellectual

tickled

domino

ignite

legacy

splurge

neigh

cabbage

erode

formalize

OR *formalise

anyway

isolation

measly

apprehensive

zither

*chiefly British spelling

invoke

upshot

climate

Yankee

dim sum

moose

cuckoo

dilemma

outrageous

silver

fedora

wildcat

monstrosity

sofa

eggplant

kosher

minority

default

heroic

bombard

furtive

journal

tulip

myself

marine

cloudy

cricket

motto

torch

pamper

pleasant

robin

historical

rules

geometric

villa

midriff

teaspoon

worrywart

developer

shopaholic

magma

briefcase

deputy

mangrove

enfranchise

kiln

webisode

kangaroo

Romeo

emerge

twitchy

arrogant

normative

homework

mildew

pattern

coffee

botch

receptacle

bagpipe

bonfire

abruptly

bushel

skedaddle

toddler

everglades

pellet

klutz

envoy

postpone

wafer

software

factoid

marvelous

OR marvellous

evince

season

horizon

arborio

cartoon

dough

emperor

utterable

leniency

frivolous

potato

wholehearted

metadata

farewell

hypnotic

jewel

tangible

nourish

vulpine

aloha

entrance

kindergarten

restaurant

excavating

dodge

iota

gelato

hankering

esteem

knack

satisfactory

barefoot

trope

knock

whittle

joyful

genuine

recluse

shield

tiger

romaine

migraine

oasis

navigator

humane

polenta

delicacy

noggin

background

thistle

althorn

Spaniel

kilt

whirlybird

Hungary

welding

aforesaid

varnish

spindle

wheedle

whelp

yonder

riffraff

restive

various

giggle

bowie

teemed

soppiness

bask

lateral

usher

prone

selfie

skydiving

memes

nuggets

frailty

sweltering

scrounge

praise

scripture

ulna

fellowship

amass

missive

jitterbug

kennel

heavenly

shindig

melody

membership

oblong

yammer

whereas

coercive

bailiff

infiltrate

skirmish

constituent

flounder

cleave

millionaire

concrete

slurry

heiress

reign

spectral

dialect

heist

avenue

pending

ewe

stagestruck

standee

sailage

yoo-hoo

profiteer

kernel

tawny

scalp

scrapple

nominee

martial

acumen

infirm

bleary

attitude

beseech

sunseeker

cornily

contraction

scooter

acceptance

rugby

shore

yippee

wand

Merlin

carnation

neaten

depose

frock

camcorder

gossip

version

fluid

vlogging

diversity

spangled

barbie

delta

handyman

stewardship

gruel

groom

trice

brick

privet

debunk

ballad

chide

atonement

citation

hardtack

rabid

teenagers

peat

harrowing

hobble

peddle

effortless

moped

groats

Highlands

***retriever

anime

regiment

sterling

bootless

forgeable

transmissibility

gridiron

summoned

***Beginning at this point, all the words remaining in the One Bee section are new to the 2022 version of *Words of the Champions*.

applicable

isms

tentacled

exude

bermudas

amusement

baptismal

postural

refrigerant

surly

scornfully

leaven

blurb

elasticity

quantify

redemption

zygote

lithium

docket

rubric

Hawaiian

pendragon

eggcorn

tabulate

cidery

puritan

caboodle

Godspeed

Thailand

pepita

lithophone

tai chi

parasol

screeno

provenance

ouster

Dudley

dicey

turken

riddance

repentant

manacle

Amish

unremitting

condiments

vaccination

floridly

obsolete

kodak

terrarium

posterity

statusy

mambo

putrid

FLOTUS

insomnia

incompetent

Disneyfication

congeniality

intertidal

solitude

optician

gelatinous

gotcha

capitalist

respite

eighth

Shetland

causal

hologram

spiteful

snitch

maternity

bungee

periwinkle

entreat

peninsular

flipperling

fleeciness

escapade

handle

gumption

mortician

homesteader

nitrate

joinery

literally

medusa

unchristened

buzzworthy

recumbent

tiffany

musketeers

windbaggery

proposal

weaponry

deceitful

cinderella

league

repercussion

astounding

hijab

donatee

parvo

apparel

squeamish

Oceanian

charitable

physical

punily

Bengal

evacuees

linguistics

pulpit

plummet

addle

Difficulty Level: Two Bee

School Spelling Bee Study List

cleat

bustling

scarf

surface

Nile

scrolls

shimmery

indent

sitcom

detect

blindfolded

basically

squints

s'mores

clobbered

relative

cringed

drone

rattled

indie

eyesore

playlist

throat

hull

outright

squabbling

scuba

trickster

glib

sneer

absent

texture

scuffle

irregular

**savor

OR savour

hedgehog

stoats

talons

inclined

wardrobe

**preferred spelling

revved

dire

masthead

vibrant

wizard

nudged

Leghorn

shrine

Jamestown

pineapple

crockery

gauze

exception

cavity

Neptune

notification

ogre

simplicity

lavished

archduke

dingoes

passersby

nada

Juneteenth

parsnips

curtains

adorned

loneliness

caverns

novice

invasions

dedicated

symbol

reduce

destination

ostriches

grudgingly

canopy

scrawny

classified

telescope

fidgeting

mulberry

surrounded

associated

furthermore

weird

dependable

summit

conkers

mutual

dormitories

tuxedo

decimal

alibi

orientation

inlaid

cobblestone

devious

sardine

contraption

technique

flaxen

triplicate

emboldened

Javas

biome

Wales

Avalon

corridor

cardigan

columns

cubicle

interjected

withered

cambric

hackles

faltered

Lincoln

granite

radiation

wattles

tartan

surveyed

emitting

preened

wretched

contorted

charlotte

elation

expanse

chai

metropolis

mousse

contessa

acutely

granules

pedestals

wreaked

renowned

colleagues

invigorating

sudoku

dutifully

mournful

professional

exerts

arid

deceptively

sustenance

Difficulty Level: Two Bee

Words of the Champions

hexagonal

litmus

seethe

antiquarian

phalanges

bachelorette

frontier

unctuous

fluoride

moorage

Minotaur

intermezzo

edification

vacuousness

epilepsy

importunate

recuperation

citronella

palliative

abhorrence

personnel

vexatious

faux

sophisticated

nebulous

genus

legionnaire

sternutation

subcutaneous

alacrity

choreographer

leguminous

ceramics

mimetic

unabated

petrifying

specimen

interlocutor

machete

dulcet

salubrious

rotisserie

**paneer

OR panir

omnibus

biscotti

calibrate

appellation

duodenum

valorous

OR *valourous

isotopic

carpal

quizzical

heliotrope

squander

prenuptial

succulent

bedraggled

rectitude

uranium

inundate

*chiefly British spelling
**preferred spelling

wunderkind

filial

wearisome

visage

fascinator

testimony

beaucoup

banal

seismologist

spectacles

innovator

bursary

hallowed

apogee

hiatus

freesia

exoneration

duvet

turpitude

platitude

nobiliary

commerce

keratitis

honorific

OR *honourific

kookaburra

napoleon

superlative

oxygenate

annihilate

sarcophagus

surrogate

terabyte

uncouth

onerous

macrocosm

bulbous

umpirage

heredity

philharmonic

endorphin

*chiefly British spelling

pharmacy

fondant

cupola

herbaceous

tentativeness

pachinko

decrepitude

redux

dramaturgy

murmuration

Clydesdale

phonics

calisthenics

obediential

odiferous

combination

torrent

arsenic

invertebrate

bandanna

OR bandana

manipulable

axiomatic

indefatigable

ulterior

oligarchy

pianola

dignify

allegiance

basaltic

scorpion

planetarium

ecstatic

cinnamon

pharaoh

opponency

referendum

quaver

rabbinic

lapel

mackerel

callow

biscuit

flourish

beatific

repository

dissipate

accomplice

kerchief

whimsical

stamina

criteria

reprieve

consequent

contusion

mulligan

sabermetrics

elocution

dowager

comparison

diaphanous

agoraphobia

buffet

tortoise

surmountable

endure

bonobo

abrogate

effusive

primitive

fabulist

comportment

taciturn

sophomoric

laureate

Goliath

splenetic

legato

slovenly

aerobics

paisley

contrariwise

petroleum

regalia

incinerate

flagon

incoherent

tercentenary

vituperative

churlish

riviera

laconic

excision

emblazoned

bric-a-brac

longitude

maverick

retrograde

partridge

insignia

binomial

luminance

adjective

elucidate

spatula

triglycerides

stalwart

bumptious

farcical

ghastly

parkour

fealty

perilous

steroid

gullibility

tarantula

cantankerous

vitriolic

crinoline

debris

armaments

versatile

subtlety

hangar

verbena

zirconium

ventriloquy

circumflex

calligram

eczema

theomachy

fibula

aberration

necrotic

eminent

demographics

Jurassic

myoglobin

frugal

achromatic

miscible

soprano

cutis

hyrax

truncheon

educand

Realtor

billabong

bariatrics

throughout

propulsion

assailant

charioteer

solicit

melismatic

spurious

tempeh

statistician

ibuprofen

injurious

anglophile

defiant

substitute

quiddity

karst

Brigadoon

vestibule

ballyhooed

arpeggio

lupine

resuscitate

approbatory

catalepsy

labyrinthine

notoriety

subterranean

aubergine

jalapeño

attributive

plutonomy

lobotomy

assumption

entrepreneur

besieged

placoderm

hermitage

permutation

conference

woebegone

resplendence

aphasia

environs

celebratory

cornucopia

prominent

archetype

travails

antipathy

leviathan

alpaca

duress

eucalyptus

rambunctious

ingenuous

phonetician

macular

simpatico

adhesion

rennet

pinnacle

avalanche

cadge

exodus

philosophize

Requiem

glitterati

transference

uveal

candelabrum

vacillate

phenotype

transposable

thrasonical

trepanation

Holstein

quadrillion

tardigrade

varsity

scholarship

filbert

Galahad

jadeite

peripheral

elevator

chaperonage

frittata

vandalize

chancellor

pauper

epoch

dumbwaiter

allergenic

vocabulary

vassal

panary

tangerine

pervasive

haphazard

legislature

shenanigans

inclusion

physicists

tempura

reggae

futility

untenable

feudalism

malevolent

posada

acquiesce

apothecary

summary

brogue

suet

koto

jingoism

satchel

evanescent

diverge

exemplar

marsupial

trefoil

designer

leisure

vague

wharf

altercation

fratority

cataclysmic

metatarsal

bereavement

carbohydrates

sesame

palatable

gratis

nonvolatile

juvenilia

fomentation

reprisal

astrobleme

sabotage

absolution

rutabaga

espousal

virulence

allocable

effraction

limousine

drupiferous

organelle

osprey

elusive

disproportionate

cayenne

tabernacle

phosphorescent

anxiety

conch

singultus

impromptu

oracle

condemn

scenographer

neuroticism

cannoli

platoon

solstice

swannery

probative

oblique

buoyancy

situation

lumbar

topiary

reverberant

yeanling

homicide

graphologist

principality

Nostradamus

taxonomic

beret

talisman

impecunious

reciprocity

molecule

millennial

ineffable

abnegation

beguile

centenary

matrimony

errata

stipulate

naïveté

cadence

fido

vehicular

sabbatical

ermine

pugilist

tapioca

festooned

tectonic

wizened

tomfoolery

harrumph

embezzlement

fallacy

asylum

remuneration

expostulate

integument

Hebrides

macaw

perspicacious

reimbursable

jambalaya

geriatric

striation

Appaloosa

ramifications

temerity

egress

geocaching

instigate

obscure

muchacha

steppe

palpitant

nonchalance

realm

estuary

technician

dietetic

homage

cumulus

essential

seraphic

cameist

scrumptiously

toploftical

noctambulist

visibility

ligament

plenitude

illustrious

symmetrical

pendulous

analepsis

mitigative

pyrite

sacrifice

consternation

escalator

impasto

antagonistic

affront

element

desolate

truncate

pedicure

**caftan

OR kaftan

ingratiate

sousaphone

amalgam

carnage

turmeric

zoolatry

ricochet

hackneyed

**preferred spelling

vespertine

**brusque

OR brusk

erstwhile

lolled

osteopath

kaiser

imperious

Egyptian

foible

lousicide

ewer

curfew

schism

dilapidated

peony

urgency

bifurcate

drivel

jettison

Promethean

**preferred spelling

embassy

contemptuous

okapi

welterweight

scrooge

morose

osmosis

flimflammer

astringent

mademoiselle

nouveau

heterochromia

consul

hermetically

excursion

dreadlocks

theriatrics

cumbersome

affluent

chastise

colic

atomic

fêng shui

acuity

subliminal

charismatic

phoenix

bastion

edamame

porcelain

deglaciation

recruit

tableau

sheldrake

suitable

cenotaph

Plumeria

perpetrator

cinematic

wallaby

contrivance

suffrage

thyme

phlebotomy

anemic

OR anaemic

depravity

effervescent

soirée

churros

diadem

larceny

acetaminophen

parochial

earnestly

**gaffe

OR gaff

ostensibly

nervily

gingivitis

patience

**preferred spelling

quittance

tenement

soothsayer

varicose

adage

cicada

mauve

emeritus

suture

obfuscate

casualty

perseverance

apparatus

myopic

ebullience

clairvoyance

impetus

affianced

archaism

commodious

austere

severance

financier

wildebeest

asado

limpa

adolescence

menagerie

hallucinate

opprobrious

nocturnal

redolent

vendage

entente

boomslang

circuitous

veracity

marionette

Neapolitan

chintzy

genteel

requisition

stimuli

schooner

declamatory

embryo

languorous

stevia

phycology

malaise

staid

acerbity

inimical

kaleidoscope

gluttonous

gypsum

polypeptide

wushu

contradictory

penitentiary

umbrage

crustaceans

bubonic

sartorial

escarpment

Celsius

dialysis

humidistat

sardonic

braille

vignette

adjudicate

caricature

emerald

liege

wilco

germane

bacteriolytic

rhododendron

ineptitude

academese

registrar

alma mater

comedienne

cutaneous

gnarled

hydroponic

combustible

factorial

dolma

sapphire

prevenient

Edenic

tributary

laudatory

jitney

wattage

papillon

vertigo

accumulate

deltoidal

opulent

paramecium

monochrome

facade

evaporation

bittern

flotsam

discombobulate

scrutiny

concatenate

impeachable

residue

halibut

spectrometer

circadian

servitude

traverse

tungsten

vineyard

interrogative

scullery

tiramisu

exaggerate

enoki

profundity

mantra

escarole

nanotechnology

bureau

burglarious

cryptozoa

preponderance

bruxism

psychoanalysis

calendar

reiterate

remorseful

cybernetics

garniture

twilight

proletarian

vantage

discountenance

stupefy

irrevocable

trellis

juxtapose

hydrangea

slalom

corollary

étude

cranium

equivalent

portentous

nepotism

truffle

varicella

tonsillitis

thoracic

proviso

netiquette

paucity

doldrums

slumgullion

valedictorian

auspices

elaborative

proprietary

seclusion

adieu

tenaciously

indemnity

cyanosis

regurgitate

stegosaur

statuesque

nectarine

galvanize

agonistic

rosin

burial

bulwark

iridescent

quince

cyclone

usurper

phraseology

caramel

pecuniary

cornea

resilience

apiary

ronin

tropical

pontiff

omniscient

capacity

sewage

epoxy

discreetly

sieve

trounce

hydrophobia

ingot

nubuck

jocularity

unfurl

calculator

corduroy

encore

hollyhock

qualms

mosaic

centipede

attendee

nomenclature

botany

Holocaust

augment

acoustic

eruption

auburn

virtually

glissando

stomach

demonstrative

megalomaniac

posse

declension

berserk

cathedral

deciduous

baleen

Einstein

municipal

adversaria

turbinado

brethren

tympanum

fisticuffs

propinquity

epidermis

carriage

abstemious

echinoderm

optimum

pathogen

acrostic

anthropology

cruciferous

macchiato

ancillary

toile

plaudits

serenade

heptad

engineer

pilcrow

porosity

tandoori

succumb

fervently

divestiture

roseola

installation

harbinger

raptatorial

sobriety

manumit

dentifrice

collegiality

inclement

celery

idiosyncratic

burgoo

occupancy

coriander

amnesty

condensation

aqueduct

ferret

widdershins

hostile

subsequent

whet

blatant

pyramid

terminus

agitation

tremulous

scythe

duplicitous

protectorate

placards

corral

credulity

dissonance

shoji

auditorium

reconcilable

evaluate

mastodon

denticulate

supplicate

torsion

justiciable

vernal

aardvark

census

stagflation

brontophobia

macrobiotics

glareous

rejuvenate

tubular

dodecahedron

rictus

vengeance

modular

kleptocrat

neuropathy

surrealist

secession

digression

intricate

annotate

vehemence

fervorous

septennial

hypotenuse

emancipatory

supine

fracas

disrepair

photogenic

rehearsal

irritability

vainglorious

ataxia

pageantry

vinegar

fiduciary

emulsify

lorikeet

malfeasance

sequential

intersperse

numerology

Paleozoic

funnel

syndicate

chrysalis

bethesda

cartilage

coeval

curio

ombudsman

hydrant

zeppelin

superficiality

marooned

volary

OR volery

follicle

brochure

grotesqueness

privatim

eradicate

krypton

ethanol

quadriceps

tachycardia

triceratops

sandal

pashmina

utilitarian

millivolt

herringbone

orchestra

phlox

tractability

montage

compendium

unmoored

yardang

fluctuation

flabbergast

accolade

connivery

impresario

bruschetta

dictum

premonition

stereotypical

bergamot

telepathic

banquet

upbraid

pancreas

expunge

maize

metastasize

quintessential

pollutant

brouhaha

pedantry

performance

equivocate

fission

boondoggle

phylum

hypochondria

obstetrician

replete

raucous

Brandywine

surreptitious

surplus

impediment

revenant

topgallant

clandestine

genealogical

pomposity

neonatology

pituitary

fleetness

anonymity

carcinogenic

detritus

anorak

enviable

extrapolate

extinguish

pilaster

perceptible

dystopia

muesli

crux

wordmonger

wobbulator

mahogany

moribund

recriminatory

subaqueous

recusancy

retrocedence

cauterize

immolate

résumé

extensive

transcend

freneticism

merino

pestilence

mordant

posthumous

QWERTY

foosball

accentuate

ascension

venue

microfiche

quadrilateral

turpentine

cellophane

indulgent

occipital

predicament

provincial

antithesis

gouge

salivate

laity

indolent

documentary

bromide

algae

reminiscent

menial

Moroccan

clearance

assure

compatriots

liaise

quotidian

matriculation

revulsive

gaucho

capsule

tragedian

fajitas

felonious

palatial

Mecca

albeit

vermicide

echelon

supremacy

clowder

occultation

Chihuahua

promontory

shar-pei

narcoleptic

efface

sycophant

bellwether

clarinet

capillary

disposition

remonstrance

smithereens

curator

judicious

vice versa

exercise

civet

pancetta

waiver

decennial

dynamite

Gemini

retinol

corpulent

potpourri

pallor

Yorkshire

Belgravia

casserole

semester

sacrament

terra-cotta

moratorium

cognizant

OR *cognisant

languish

protuberant

chortle

*chiefly British spelling

unscathed

raclette

superstitious

mawkish

flambé

patronymic

odometer

uvula

enumerated

desertification

quirky

arraign

elegant

minacious

vindictive

implacable

logarithmic

regicide

hubris

hibernaculum

bandicoot

malinger

parliamentary

rebarbative

olympiad

crocodile

venerable

chemise

campanology

persuasible

desultorily

papyrus

El Niño

anchorage

conundrum

debilitate

mittimus

mellifluous

clemency

backgammon

intuitable

divvy

fatuously

fraudulent

necessity

piety

veritable

sashay

sciatica

discomfiture

emphysema

stridency

acetone

cerebellum

pantomime

prima donna

praxis

Tinseltown

sorrel

McCoy

histrionics

cashier

polysemy

stampede

forfeit

armadillo

overweening

sacrosanct

syringe

eclipse

espadrille

corgi

caffeine

panacea

cabaret

froufrou

eschew

ventricle

inducement

vanguard

portrait

tepidity

meridian

spontaneity

platinum

nonnegotiable

disparate

artifice

cymbals

nucleated

exorbitant

reparations

constabulary

speculate

stratosphere

noxious

arbitrary

quasar

Podunk

seize

pathos

equinox

prosperous

sclerosis

ablaut

anabolic

jimberjawed

toilsome

tempestuous

univocal

avarice

bouclé

thoroughbred

potassium

peculate

treatise

undergird

oompah

adulation

minutia

anticipatory

chinook

indigent

merganser

sternum

par excellence

thwartwise

tae kwon do

fenestrated

lugubrious

isosceles

hoity-toity

Mesopotamian

Muzak

vicinity

merely

abominable

procedure

limpid

syllabus

animus

trillium

Dalmatian

ufology

cholera

**minuscule

OR miniscule

jeepney

volucrine

populace

vetiver

parameters

inflammable

pyrotechnics

mollify

cohesive

stigmata

prolix

**preferred spelling

mitochondria

onomatopoeia

lavender

tensile

gaudery

luxuriate

cavalcade

gladiatorial

machination

pugnacious

peruse

alluvial

epicurean

derelict

revelation

arithmetic

depredation

ignominious

auction

assiduous

diligence

bodega

bona fide

gustatory

obliterate

legalese

rudiments

monitory

equilibrium

roustabout

trifle

ambrosial

simultaneity

gastronome

epithet

encroach

acacia

tetanus

scarlatina

ciao

genome

inviolable

contrite

patrician

enervate

turophile

Patagonia

vanquish

ectoplasm

olfactory

en masse

stroganoff

procrastinate

purification

plantain

aperture

rhythmically

shazam

bountiful

pantheon

marimba

conduit

bravado

beneficent

indict

epitome

annulment

vegetarian

surimi

besmirch

trespass

commandeer

bonsai

university

celestial

preposterous

extant

cogently

auricular

settee

legitimately

inoculate

heleoplankton

pliant

billiards

obstreperous

frabjous

spiracle

Formica

Mylar

rustication

globular

stellular

akimbo

derisive

ineluctable

eerily

funambulist

apotheosis

entrée

homeostasis

mummified

prehensile

somatotype

bizarro

dissemble

gallant

intensify

hurriedly

corrosive

afghan

odontiasis

stratification

tomahawk

artesian

mendacious

gubernatorial

pungent

mandrill

gibbous

extracurricular

punctuation

nautilus

thievery

dragoon

yuzu

ritziness

gazette

continuum

pachyderm

symposium

floribunda

salience

molasses

classical

fungible

Gothamite

affable

dopamine

pitiful

ammunition

pariah

prodigious

denominator

prorogue

fecund

laceration

nexus

decor

duchy

pagoda

establishment

ruminate

sympathy

puniness

lingua franca

triforium

**déjà vu

OR déjà vue

calabash

**chute

OR shute

impermeable

trepidation

collision

scarab

veganism

humerus

vagabonds

variegated

volition

gossamer

vincible

factitious

sculpture

annuity

quid pro quo

**preferred spelling

curmudgeon

cushion

tutelage

domiciled

theorem

accrual

grandeur

ottoman

logographic

armistice

cryogenic

catalyst

thespian

submersible

extemporaneous

ungetatable

unilaterally

ordinance

ursine

arduous

carnitas

bulgogi

fibromyalgia

terrier

captivated

onus

precursor

mochi

feign

dementia

voilà

habanero

Francophone

convivium

atrium

italicization

preliminary

echoed

reticulated

authenticate

fiscal

oblige

viscount

plague

preferential

bazooka

complacency

kraken

stanzaic

putrescent

nostalgia

dechlorinate

unconscionable

Pembroke

liquefaction

palazzo

miasma

concoct

modicum

javelin

spoonerism

complicit

gyrocopter

**medieval

OR mediaeval

licensure

Herculean

pilgrimages

oriel

preeminent

alfresco

loquacious

prosthetic

latency

epitaphs

solitaire

dishevel

Limburger

tuffet

epact

abstruse

**preferred spelling

nephrolith

adipose

quorum

pharynx

epistolary

pursuit

esoteric

grapheme

trigonometry

alloy

Belgium

audacious

exasperate

Mandarin

Kelvin

vellum

enunciate

tarsier

autodidact

parable

rowan

tripartite

Bohemian

succinct

inquietude

compunction

decumbiture

multivalent

artillery

quotient

ricotta

guttural

atrocious

vivacious

xenoglossy

smorgasbord

electrode

sporadically

sudation

cytoplasm

affectionately

Pulitzer

vitreous

wraith

insulin

phlegmatic

spasmodic

bouquet

denizen

duopoly

alpinist

abracadabra

plethora

rappelled

conceit

tapas

sediment

emulate

caveat

doubloons

oscillation

enzyme

dinero

comestibles

stenographer

mezzanine

lozenge

tedious

resonate

suspicion

repudiate

emporium

Victorian

forestallment

Iberian

dandle

effete

Antigua

vaudeville

frisket

brockage

malapropism

pelf

aqueous

Dianthus

olingo

Halifax

concordance

huerta

vascular

wentletrap

serrated

poblano

conclave

Gregorian

rebuff

taverna

illicitly

cribbage

crith

Namibian

tricenary

triste

interred

legerity

Vatican

fucoid

parley

meningitis

nutation

nutria

sedge

capstan

vicarious

alate

victimology

ibex

cudgel

bicameral

irrigation

labradoodle

portico

corsage

smellfungus

arboretum

Zamboni

blarney

diacritic

mephitic

complementary

Philistine

dyspeptic

inglorious

louche

avatar

grandiloquent

armature

maidenhair

aureole

spinosity

prespinous

cladistics

gasiform

valuator

deserter

jankers

Evactor

possessive

venial

seton

demerits

diaspora

pious

borough

volatile

gnocchi

surety

pileus

fez

glengarry

commissioner

grande dame

verism

dramatization

nonconformist

château

erroneous

Salvador

trillado

per se

peradventure

Ryeland

domesticity

episcopal

consecrate

trituration

neoterism

interregnum

viaticum

homiletics

psalmody

omnilegent

princeps

procurement

cribo

colubrine

immie

aretalogy

sessile

du jour

lanceolate

bowsprit

Charon

chupacabra

Acadians

Gippsland

froward

ensconced

cattalo

OR catalo

hypogeous

***composite

Miranda

Newfoundland

fulminate

bilaterian

wootz

movimento

mandorla

pomegranate

parodic

osculatory

orthogonal

planisphere

tase

Shiba Inu

misnomer

eustress

blastogenesis

octuplicate

in silico

***Beginning at this point, all the words remaining in the Two Bee section are new to the 2022 version of *Words of the Champions*.

particulate

planogram

Pomeranian

freegan

emissary

balsamic

pothos

polysyllabic

teraphim

anserine

elicitation

advocatory

eligibility

placate

runcible spoon

goji berry

implicative

sostenuto

credence

Farsi

novemdecillion

adjugate

epidural

patella

hydrocortisone

maritime

debutante

ramson

asthmatic

pilosity

depreciate

Pierre

davenport

convocation

recreant

majuscule

Cheshire cat

phishing

Motrin

tsk-tsked

cum laude

evo-devo

lumen

catalina

Sumatran

restitutory

cholesterol

astaxanthin

Florentine

stricture

no-goodnik

agnail

perquisite

pilotage

arietta

deprivation

ante

amiably

nomancy

officinal

Cassandra

quinary

afroth

rhapsody

Franciscan

abaft

Romano

impoverish

flexitarian

parsimony

prion

ancho

polyester

anoint

appraisal

parabola

primeval

morphological

retrodict

expectorant

Tasmanian

hipsterism

melamine

eluate

heterophony

polonium

espial

kung pao

aglossal

nodosity

somniloquy

antacid

umbilical

zacate

acquit

capnometer

fontina

biomimicry

durango

pomato

inerrancy

Munich

coalition

discretionary

inveterate

Difficulty Level: Three Bee

School Spelling Bee Study List

reflexology

intentionally

cocoon

motley

fetlocks

ranchero

intolerance

gluten

pulverized

OR *pulverised

mystified

swankiest

clouting

demeanor

OR *demeanour

mallet

Singapore

disembodied

Korea

aisles

unsportsmanlike

ensnarement

morbidity

proctors

trodden

torturous

referral

aerials

surgeon

Judaism

stalemate

thoroughfare

transgressions

abdomen

appeasement

liability

penchant

propensity

instinctive

infectious

Minnesota

adversity

convictions

intestine

discriminating

exile

lineage

coaxing

permanence

larkspur

drudgery

ransacked

**kimchi

OR kimchee

menorahs

heirloom

pallid

renal

mete

russet

topologically

burgundy

brocade

**preferred spelling

heresy

perdition

incorrigibles

porcine

dispensation

Richter scale

palpable

congealing

bantlings

prioress

embroidery

coronation

padre

mien

resinous

scree

chaplain

feinted

humus

Cantonese

herbalist

fortuitous

poultice

guarantor

adduced

impertinent

fractious

Darwinism

transept

condescendingly

rhetorical

phenomenal

mortification

covenant

throes

semblance

aversion

primordial

moppet

assassinate

vuvuzela

adzuki

allée

d'orsay

Wiesbaden

Montmorency

justaucorps

ducats

condyles

Yom Kippur

Firenze

kaddish

Chelonia

Quasimodo

Helvetia

lachrymose

quatrains

katabatic

bivouac

fata morgana

hawsers

Bayreuth

vambrace

plastron

linsey-woolsey

Albion

paschal

coracle

abalones

repast

Bloomsbury

aquiline

Confucianism

Chaucerian

Edinburgh

Carlisle

Mantua

Jains

ziggurat

Arapaho

OR Arapahoe

Durham

derrick

Kerala

chandleries

bier

Des Moines

conurbation

Sioux

refectory

presidio

imaret

cornichon

devastavit

Mediterranean

longevous

digerati

solecism

hypertrophy

ravigote

inchoate

judoka

vaccary

Adelaide

unwonted

tazza

damson

pelisse

succade

tumulus

dorsiflexor

profiterole

valetudinary

aristoi

vireo

rococo

lachsschinken

wakame

bathos

nihilism

ustion

sumpsimus

morel

abeyance

rongeur

mountebank

allelopathy

capoeira

agnolotti

ballabile

draegerman

prescient

Fribourg

proselytizer

OR *proselytiser

tenon

nubilous

iatrogenic

onychitis

roux

tuatara

chicle

sulcus

thalamus

gyttja

jibboom

vestigial

Orwellian

gimbaled

OR gimballed

cabaletta

hesped

umami

*chiefly British spelling

persiflage

toreador

vermicelli

frangipane

reseau

moulage

interpellate

genuflect

cinerarium

polemic

paladin

totipotency

agnomen

Bauhaus

sacerdotal

skeuomorph

binturong

mamushi

lipophilic

codicil

coulomb

violaceous

Rorschach

arthralgia

desman

jacaranda

huapango

predilection

entomophagy

paronomasia

facsimile

renminbi

interferon

sedulous

velouté

Aesopian

frigate

enoptromancy

satiety

perorate

danseur

chevalier

taurine

hierurgical

melee

emolument

ikebana

exaugural

gaillardia

caryatid

heliacal

schefflera

contrapposto

temblor

insouciance

catarrh

quattrocento

millegrain

canaille

verisimilitude

Keynesian

akaryote

azulejo

hauberk

bouillon

tarpaulin

cephalopod

pulchritude

pekoe

patois

Rubicon

Truckee

aerophilatelic

ankh

contumelious

vicissitudes

lilliputian

Sbrinz

kathakali

cozen

oxalis

myeloma

lebensraum

mufti

dirigible

surcease

ascetic

oolite

revanche

megrims

podagra

palaver

luthier

yttriferous

vermeil

Ouagadougou

bibliopegist

plagiarism

holobenthic

boutonniere

anodyne

saccharide

boulevardier

quokka

lidocaine

contretemps

a posteriori

scaberulous

anaglyphy

reconnoiter

OR reconnoitre

realpolitik

colloque

onychorrhexis

existence

vigneron

tannined

spiedini

anhinga

jai alai

Rastafarian

succussion

avifauna

joropo

toxicosis

**colporteur

OR colporter

agitprop

Achernar

cassock

meringue

mackinaw

sambal

yuloh

hermeneutics

tikkun

macaque

lassitude

oeuvre

altazimuth

Castilian

**preferred spelling

trichinosis

ecclesiology

teppanyaki

cicatrize

somnolent

intonaco

realia

grison

phulkari

garrulous

paroxysm

communiqué

Chantilly

jacquard

sorghum

guilloche

appositive

dirndl

latke

martinet

asterion

hypallage

solenoid

veridical

threnody

Jacobean

ballotage

ocotillo

dubitante

disciform

mizuna

trichotillomania

huipil

mustelid

prestidigitation

soupçon

diphtheria

bdelloid

nugatory

commorients

immiscible

toroidal

bialy

appurtenances

corsair

zabaglione

velamen

sporran

clematis

kente

ranine

riparian

**accoutrement

OR accouterment

radicchio

dudgeon

nitid

Basenji

concinnate

Stradivarius

synecdoche

**preferred spelling

tulsi

sebaceous

papeterie

litigious

phytophilous

meunière

hilum

fanfaronade

malachite

urticaria

capsaicin

ptosis

pejerrey

horologist

speleothem

euripus

samarium

variscite

bolide

vervain

chanoyu

hamadryad

calumny

escabeche

ad hominem

oubliette

béchamel

repoussage

otacoustic

naranjilla

elegiac

pâtissier

Yeatsian

surfeit

limicolous

girandole

googol

étagère

anechoic

leonine

laulau

Gruyère

proprioceptive

oppugn

macropterous

euphonious

retinoscopy

sepulchral

sangfroid

pasilla

maringouin

argot

vicenary

ajimez

pompeii

oviparous

mangonel

coalescence

Plantagenet

bauxite

kakapo

pelagial

ague

largesses

fulgent

olecranon

toreutics

mascarpone

rissole

seneschal

pinniped

wahine

grissino

coterie

sylph

Cincinnati

diastole

mediobrome

demurrage

tristeza

trigeminal

bruja

upsilon

sakura

buccal

zocalo

**aficionado

OR afficionado

piscivorous

benison

gagaku

amygdala

scurrilous

flèche

tetrachoric

sforzando

thalassic

frazil

rapprochement

glacis

**preferred spelling

ahimsa

kanji

weltschmerz

jalousie

ichthyology

pruritus

dactylic

affogato

scrivener

dysrhythmia

dragée

choucroute

hsaing-waing

stevedore

harangue

niveau

rouille

rescissible

Jungian

Groenendael

facile

chrysolite

execrable

hangul

cartouches

Nicoise

julienne

moiety

pastitsio

modiste

deuterium

Icarian

pappardelle

Sahel

bibelot

telegnosis

loupe

oleiculture

**loess

OR löss

ruelle

**preferred spelling

Ushuaia

redingote

adscititious

hummock

internecine

duxelles

mesial

Feldenkrais

bailiwick

bozzetto

coiffure

repartee

chimera

OR *chimaera

avgolemono

exiguous

presentient

renvoi

kichel

semaphore

gambol

angiitis

Teutonic

Conestoga

zeitgeist

heinousness

nacelle

rupicolous

Pythagorean

kepi

**bulgur

OR bulghur

ushabti

puchero

nival

ascites

Véronique

planetesimal

taoiseach

obeisant

whippoorwill

Ficus

**preferred spelling

agelicism

subrident

ethylene

flaneur

Ponzi

teneramente

styptic

sopapilla

nictitate

boutade

towhee

escritoire

affenpinscher

gudgeon

beaumontage

galoot

desiccate

aporia

moraine

hirsute

shubunkin

hepatectomy

bloviate

seine

galapago

au courant

crepuscular

theca

croustade

kipuka

noumenon

chicanery

vilipend

vitiate

spodumene

leberwurst

daguerreotype

yakitori

pejorate

Aitutakian

parterre

rondeau

atlatl

allochroous

ennui

caisson

cheongsam

graticule

gyascutus

cygnet

supercilious

dysphasia

kugel

topazolite

trompe l'oeil

ailette

fetticus

rocaille

couverture

lemniscus

ad nauseam

ganache

sauger

kanban

toccata

pertinacity

gasthaus

transmontane

laterigrade

hyssop

naumachia

focaccia

pahoehoe

Kjeldahl

rubefacient

halcyon

corrigenda

Zanni

nonage

beurre

jicama

sturnine

octonocular

parallax

antenatus

trouvaille

glazier

kinesiology

exogenous

aniseikonia

guayabera

realgar

anaphylaxis

bobolink

diluent

urushiol

andouille

otiose

megacephalic

souchong

poltroon

Freudian

floruit

Bunyanesque

exsect

champignon

bahuvrihi

panjandrum

catachresis

tiffin

colcannon

tournedos

ormolu

blottesque

consommé

ullage

zortzico

teratism

flagellum

panegyric

hoi polloi

sirenian

nescience

blatherskite

consigliere

adiabatic

camembert

ecchymosis

oppidan

decastich

Naugahyde

lefse

beccafico

amphistylar

saturnine

zaibatsu

titian

tokonoma

unguiculate

amaryllis

reveille

regnal

attaché

rafflesia

ranunculus

pistou

scintillation

Bolognese

farrago

coup de grace

tourelle

notturno

ginglymus

hemorrhage

tapetum

golem

krewe

toque

avuncular

habiliments

rubato

gentilitial

obnebulate

allonym

croquembouche

kobold

mendicity

castellated

toponymic

boudin

bucatini

reboation

haupia

Keplerian

codswallop

hauteur

camarilla

nidicolous

oxyacetylene

Humboldt

hellebore

transhumance

phloem

lacustrine

ageusia

pillor

deleterious

ikat

pylorus

erythroblast

maillot

epenthesis

hinoki

nonpareil

nyctinasty

pointelle

vinaigrette

tinnient

aioli

pochoir

glyceraldehyde

hagiographer

syncope

icosahedron

goanna

wassail

ammonite

tanager

pneumatocyst

fortissimo

portmanteau

coaxation

ardoise

farouche

farfalle

ogival

stretto

coccygeal

Diplodocus

tachyon

piccata

isagoge

élan

breviloquence

kalimba

illative

betony

bêtise

transience

frison

flavedo

maquillage

mortadella

stanchion

spirulina

eleemosynary

force majeure

ossicle

anemone

alpargata

disembogue

luculent

expatiate

xerogel

vizierial

crescive

tryptophan

neophyte

buffa

clavichord

de rigueur

secant

comanchero

meiosis

gules

nimiety

lokelani

psoriasis

bavardage

coulibiac

xyloglyphy

Aramaic

anathema

basilica

rajpramukh

Chalcolithic

rinceau

filar

bhangra

risorgimento

agalma

analgesia

dengue

cantatrice

emollient

parquet

dhurrie

lapidary

cachexia

connoisseur

ferruginous

gendarme

demulcent

goosander

kwashiorkor

lecithin

cetology

plenipotentiary

foudroyant

sesquipedalian

expugnable

profligacy

yosenabe

funori

piloncillo

xiphias

étouffée

degauss

tussock

lanolated

linnet

embouchure

plangency

apocryphal

tamarack

puerilely

obloquy

dhole

Sangamon

outré

ululate

sororal

epideictic

embolus

caveola

farina

heuristic

nudibranch

triquetra

paramahamsa

duello

fjeld

tomography

effleurage

chastushka

bergère

Erewhonian

rhyton

orogeny

Pepysian

esplanade

gesellschaft

tamari

arenaceous

panettone

tmesis

clerihew

tsukupin

katakana

Parmentier

rugose

brume

hiortdahlite

extravasate

incunabula

cordillera

zazen

cabochon

après

zydeco

consanguine

bibimbap

aquiclude

demitasse

tomalley

bouffant

bas-relief

rhizome

Wensleydale

erubescent

estovers

rembrandt

marcel

croquignole

dolmen

griot

vexillologist

**halala

OR halalah

corybantic

chasuble

furuncle

pongee

acoel

acral

Koine

weka

haplography

Tchefuncte

becquerel

**preferred spelling

darnel

giallolino

krausen

Castalia

nahcolite

telamon

uraeus

teledu

gattine

mele

Marathi

nuciform

grandrelle

bordereaux

rambla

tullibee

guichet

Guarnerius

unakite

azotea

gabbro

gegenschein

hebdomadal

gypsophila

koh-i-noor

nocive

cataphora

blastema

trochee

diapason

deliquesce

aperçu

cioppino

inglenook

efflux

frugivore

lobscouse

senecio

jasmone

hawok

`

fructiferous

martinoe

lierre

porwigle

portugais

ligas

Osloite

sciolistic

seraya

janthina

Skeltonic

balata

balbriggan

affeer

pomology

Svengali

escheator

dogana

toorie

exchequer

habeas corpus

kerril

pudibund

toril

ryas

terai

gabarit

guerite

gallivat

charcuterie

zugzwang

triskelion

crokinole

anicca

batamote

yabbies

**salmagundi

OR salmagundy

**hutia

OR jutia

Deseret

Djibouti

**preferred spelling

Tegucigalpa

Llullaillaco

Pyxis

***Bezier curve

Beauceron

ni-Vanuatu

Vulcan

anabathmoi

selah

cirri

Oort cloud

cobalamin

amuse-gueule

anent

abaculus

Dvorak

sous vide

Nethinim

Rayleigh wave

Gaia

***Beginning at this point, all the words remaining in the Three Bee section are new to the 2022 version of *Words of the Champions*.

Ner Tamid

cathect

mange-tout

whakapapa

Astur

Casimir effect

Devanagari

bismillah

deceleron

Ardipithecus

Equatoguinean

limaçon

Kannada

Bundt

Strigolniki

Bavarian cream

hysteron proteron

rooseveltite

temalacatl

darmstadtium

Eris

flehmen

au bleu

pou sto

kapparah

Kuiper Belt

Quaoar

agate

art brut

banh mi

attacca

Ryukyu

kalopanax

derring-do

Alfvén

virga

ab aeterno

Caracas

indicia

Huallaga

kufi

Novanglian

una corda

triduum

wapiti

galena

gyokuro

luftmensch

aggrandizement

battue

Tok Pisin

dvandva

ivermectin

coulrophobia

ancien régime

deathin

zowie

colocate

Aglaia

Apostolici

ubiquinone

Gurmukhi

Burkinabe

ciliopathy

logothete

grobian

rond de jambe

kyphoplasty

Aten

catjang

neem

amour propre

Sagittarius

hordeolum

trous-de-loup

vis-à-vis

Latinxua

Barnumesque

medulla

aughts

carnitine

ahuehuete

hominin